Satisfaction

Satisfaction

The Art of
the Female Orgasm

Kim Cattrall AND Mark Levinson

Illustrations BY Fritz Drury

WARNER BOOKS

An AOL Time Warner Company

Honesty and caring are everything.

Warner Books, Inc., 1271 Avenue of the Americas, New York NY 10020

Visit our Web site at www.twbookmark.com.

WARNER BOOKS

An AOL Time Warner Company

Printed in England

Originally published in hardcover by Warner Books, Inc.

First Trade Printing: February 2003

1   3   5   7   9   10   8   6   4   2

CIP information available upon request

ISBN-0-446-69090-2

Illustrator: Fritz Drury
Designer: Midori Nakamura
Digital Imaging: Daniel Rutkowski

This book is intended for use by adults who are informed and want to invigorate and maintain a great sexual relationship. The authors are not medically trained and the reader is reminded that following these guidelines and new ideas is voluntary and at the reader's own discretion. The positions and methodology presented herein are safe and satisfying for most adult men and women, however, every individual is different and you should not undertake any position or technique that is not suitable to your physical condition. You should consult a health care professional with any questions. Certain acts described in this book are illegal in some states and you should be aware of the laws in your state.

Our deepest thanks go to the models who contributed so much to this book.

GLOSSARY OF SYMBOLS

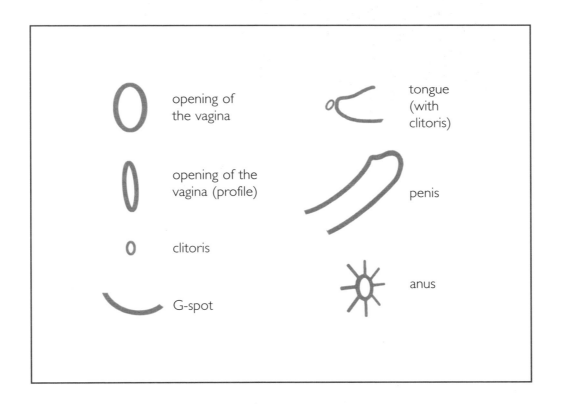

opening of the vagina

opening of the vagina (profile)

clitoris

G-spot

tongue (with clitoris)

penis

anus

Contents

Introduction

This book is not really about sex. It is about love. Loving means caring, and what is more caring than wanting our lover or mate to experience the fullest expression of his or her sexuality? Many women will privately admit that their lovers do not know how to satisfy them fully. There are men who know how to bring a woman to orgasm, even repeatedly, but they are a small minority. This book is intended to help couples achieve the deepest sexual fulfillment. However, the text and drawings in this book are of limited value without strong feelings of the heart.

Anyone can learn techniques, but technique alone will not make a person a great lover. Each man and woman has specific preferences and needs, and each must develop great sensitivity and awareness for the other to reap the full benefits of the techniques they learn. When you try adapting the material in this book, remember that your true purpose is not to simply perform a physical act; it is to enable your lover to feel things more deeply, to let him or her experience release beyond expectations, and ultimately to bring you and your partner closer together psychologically, emotionally, and spiritually.

When a man fully satisfies a woman, he frees her from harboring negative feelings such as frustration, disappointment, and anger. Men should consider what it would be like to make love without ever achieving climax. The thought alone should be inspiration to leave no stone unturned in the quest to give her the utmost pleasure when making love.

When he fulfills her, her passion will be released and
she will be naturally motivated to fulfill him.
Ultimately, both the man and the woman
will benefit from increased desire as
they both enjoy satisfaction.

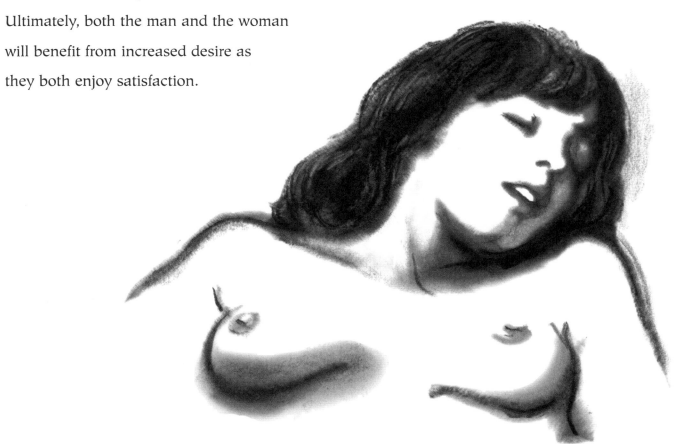

A Note from Kim

People often ask me if I'm anything like the characters I play. Some people have even said that they assumed that for me to play a sexually open character, like Samantha Jones on HBO's *Sex and the City*, I must have had fabulous sex most of my life. Well, the truth is that until three years ago most of my sexual experiences were unfulfilling.

One purpose of this book is to debunk the myth that attractive women with sexy images have fabulous sex lives. The hype and glamour surrounding show business and the people in it reinforce that fiction. The parts an actor plays may have little to do with who she really is and how she feels. Many of the roles I've played—usually sexually aware, no-nonsense gals—have had nothing to do with me or what my life is really like. Quite frankly, these false images have, at times, interfered with my relationships and personal sexual satisfaction.

In my early thirties, I lamented to a girlfriend that many of the men I had been with seemed unaware of what could lead to sexual fulfillment for both of us. She cited the Rita Hayworth scenario, suggesting that perhaps my problems were due to men feeling that they were being intimate with an image they had seen on the screen and that when the real person appeared they were either disappointed or overwhelmed. Consequently, I was disappointed and unsatisfied, too.

I talked with friends, read books written by sex therapists, and sought professional help. I stood naked in front of the mirror learning to get in touch with my body. I studied diagrams that never fully explained where and how I could

achieve orgasm with my partner. I turned forty. I'd gone through two decades of unsatisfactory sexual relationships.

I had convinced myself that I just wasn't a sexual woman, and like my mother before me, I began to feel that sex really wasn't that important. To me, sex meant being physically dominated by a man and experiencing some pleasure through the act of penetration in intercourse, but never reaching orgasm with my partners. So, I resolved to put all my energy into my work and my family, and joined my single girlfriends in their common complaint of not being able to find any good men.

Then, in January of 1998, I met my husband, Mark. Since then, I have learned many things about communication, sexuality, and honesty. I've also realized that one of the biggest limitations in sexual life is that many men don't know

how to enable a woman to reach orgasm, and many women
are not informed or confident enough to tell men what
they need to do. I've discovered that the whole subject
is essentially taboo. No one wants to admit that millions
of women have unsatisfactory sex lives and that most men
do not know what to do about it.

When friends heard that Mark and I were writing a book
about how to fulfill a woman, they first asked, "Can I get
a copy?" and then, "Why would you want to give away
all your secrets?" My response has always been this:
Why should sexual knowledge be thought of as secret?
Why should information to satisfy both sexes be hidden
or left to chance? With all the books by doctors and therapists,
why is it that so many people are still suffering from a lack
of sexual fulfillment? Information and advice about sex can
and should be shared in a clear, concise, and honest way,

and that's what Mark and I hope to contribute with this book. Our intent is to share ideas, scenarios, and suggestions that will lead people to greater mutual sexual satisfaction.

The character of Samantha Jones is a sexually free spirit who goes from man to man in an endless search for the right one. Many women say they would like to be more like Samantha, because she has a large sexual appetite and does what she wants in the bedroom. Many men see Samantha as the ideal date for the same reason. In real life, people want great sex as part of something more substantial: a partnership that comprises love, caring, and support, and provides avenues for growth and fulfillment on many different levels.

People sometimes tell me how *Sex and the City* has changed their way of thinking about sex. Samantha's openness makes people feel comfortable talking to me, Kim, about the ways in which they have experienced sexual disappointment and frustration. I find it fascinating, sad, and curiously comforting that I felt the same frustrations myself. Such experiences had made me feel quite alone, but now I realize that many women have felt this way. If you feel this way, know that you are not alone, and there is a solution!

Most men and women want the same things sexually— intimacy and deeply fulfilling sex with the one they love. But many couples have a difficult time achieving this. How then do we find sexual satisfaction?

Most of my sexual knowledge came from trial and error, but few partners knew more than I did at an early age. The female orgasm was something that other women experienced, or was induced by masturbation or the use of a vibrator. I remember once setting my cap for a known ladies' man just to get a glimpse of what I'd been missing. Let's just say that he had terrific P.R. In reality, the sex was just another disappointment.

I believe that a man should know how to make a woman experience orgasm until she is truly satisfied. This is not the only ingredient of a good relationship, but it certainly is excellent glue for binding couples closer together.

Satisfaction is not something you can get simply from a description or a drawing. These aids can function as a starting point or a springboard, but ultimately, the man must feel the woman and the woman must feel the man— in every sense of the word. Any woman who has been constantly let down by men in bed cannot expect her fear of disappointment and her anger at the years of frustration to disappear instantly. However, these feelings will melt away quickly when she begins to have orgasms and sees that her man wants her to be as fulfilled as possible. And for men, nothing compares to having your lover respond to your touch. For couples who seek this, we offer this book and hope it will be helpful.

I was quite surprised to discover how quickly my body responded to being touched in the right way. It didn't take much time to begin having orgasms. As my comfort and experience continue to deepen, so does the bond between Mark and me. When a man knows what to do, it is amazing how fast you can move on to new levels of intimacy.

Many people find it difficult to open up emotionally. Making the leap takes a combination of personal readiness, the right partner, and the right circumstances. When a man knows how to make love to a woman, it changes everything. When a woman finds herself

responding, she should let it happen and feel everything. As she does, her response will intensify as well. I used to protect myself by limiting how much I felt, but I realized it would be wiser simply to let go. For me, the process is still unfolding. I continually open up more and more— the journey never ends. The best way to show appreciation for a great lover is by responding to his touch. This is a woman's greatest gift to her man, as well as the most liberating experience for her.

My wish is for those of you who have been living with little sexual fulfillment to realize that you are not alone. There is a way to have the sexual life you want. I know because I was unsatisfied for years, and finally found a path to real satisfaction.

A Note from Mark

When I was eighteen, my first lover was a woman nine years older than myself. The first time we made love, I was very excited and really had no idea what was supposed to happen. She coached me without my knowing it, and the third time we made love she told me that she had an orgasm. I was unaware of her experience and did not know what she meant. How does a woman have an orgasm? What does she feel? Do I have anything to do with it? Can I make it happen? Why was I so unaware of her experience?

I was confused and embarrassed, and decided that I wanted to better my understanding of how women work physically and emotionally, and to become the best lover I could be.

Why didn't I just ask her some questions? Very few men are comfortable asking a woman what feels right to her, heightens her experience, and makes her climax. It seems to be something men don't generally do.

Even if a man asks, the woman may be at a loss to explain to him what to do. A woman may know how to touch herself, but very few seem to know what a man can specifically do to excite her and make her come.

Perhaps we fear that if we talk about it, the magic of the moment will go away. Well, not talking about it has created a situation that is not working for many people.

I learned a lot about sex from being with different women,

and by seeing what worked best for each person. Over

the course of time, I became more aware and intuitive,

and learned to feel my partner instinctively. It is an awareness

that must be developed, but it is available to everyone.

Everything may be right in a relationship, but if sexual

satisfaction is minimal or absent, the relationship is likely

to suffer. All show and no go is not a promising scenario.

It is amazing that in our society we have no tradition

of passing along this most basic and vital knowledge—

how to satisfy a woman. After all, when a man truly satisfies

his lover, he attains true release for himself.

Kim and I are not doctors or professional sex therapists,

but we are two people who are not afraid to talk to each other

about what brings us satisfaction in bed. We hope that

the material in this book will be helpful to those who want to be better lovers, as well as to those who want their partners to be better at lovemaking. Maybe others will write books that go beyond this one. If so, we will happily read and learn from them. At this point in time, we have not seen a book that contains this material, so we offer ours hoping for the best.

This book assumes that the man has the desire to fulfill the woman, and that the woman wants fulfillment with him. If this is not the case, this book will be of no value and other remedies should be considered.

The real purpose of this book is to help men develop their intuitive abilities and their overall consciousness and awareness of women and themselves. Ultimately, when she is sexually fulfilled, he has one of his greatest rewards.

"If your man is not an artist yet, he can become one. Once he 'gets it' and starts to feel you, be sure to show your appreciation."

— Kim

"One night, Kim said, 'You are an artist.' That was one of the greatest compliments I received in my entire life."

— Mark

Every Man Can Be an Artist

Every man can be an artist if he decides he wants to be one.
It just requires intent and practice.

The material in this book is like color on an artist's palette.
It is up to the man to paint the picture; the woman is
the inspirational guide. Each woman may like some of the
techniques in this book and not others. Each man must
adapt the material to his partner's wishes. Every man and
woman has his or her own touch, rhythms, and motions,
and each time they make love, the man can bring forth
a new experience for his partner and for himself. The key
to bringing a woman to total fulfillment is to pay attention
to what she is telling you with her breathing, her body,
and her words.

Start with the techniques at the beginning of this book and discover what works—you will know right away. There is a definite "yes" or "no" response that you can sense very quickly. Find out what creates the "yes" response and discard that which produces the "no" response.

Starting with gentleness is always best. You can easily intensify, but a rough start can derail the train. Ask her to tell you if she wants added intensity. It is more erotic to ask for more rather than less. But it is better to ask for less than to suffer. The most important thing for a man is to tune in to the woman through her responses: Is she moving toward you or pulling away? Is she lubricating more or less? Is her breathing fast and shallow or very controlled? Through these and other signs, a woman conveys her responses—and a man must be ready to listen to them.

"Someone I knew once said, 'What I am about to tell you has the added advantage of being the truth.' You can tell your lover that you disagree with his or her opinion, but you should never say that his or her feeling is wrong. Feelings can never be right or wrong. We can argue about what we think but we can only express what we feel. If we say, 'Your feeling is wrong, you can't feel that,' we risk slamming the door shut on any further communication and hitting a dead end in the relationship. Hear your lover and acknowledge that you understand. If she says, 'I feel this,' acknowledge receipt of the message. Say 'I'm glad you told me'—it goes a long way.

"It is important to remember that some people have deep fears caused by past experience that cannot be easily resolved in a casual conversation. It is helpful to create a climate of calm understanding, which supports healing."

—Mark

"A woman will often shy away from saying that she's frustrated because she is afraid of hurting a man's ego and being punished for it. With that fear present, there is little hope for the relationship at all. The only hope is to be honest, in a gentle but direct manner.

"Most men appreciate straight talk. Straight means simple and direct, not weaseling, aggressive, or bitchy. It's not easy for many women to talk about their sexual feelings and needs, but men respond best to a direct, straight-talk approach.

"If you are sexually frustrated, say something. If you don't, your anger will fester and create more problems. But make it safe for him by being gentle. For example, 'I really love you and I'd like to enjoy making love with you more. Can we try a few things?' Most men will say

'Sure. What did you have in mind?'
You can talk directly about
the material in the book
or say, 'Well, I have this
book and I'm really
excited about doing
some of these things
with you. I think
this will help me
be a better lover
for you.'"

—Kim

Fear of the Truth

Many people fear that telling the truth will hurt their lover, or result in conflict that will be extremely damaging. This is often a source of great anxiety, and is a theme that recurs in art as well as in personal life.

Sam Raimi's film *The Gift* (2000), co-written by Billy Bob Thornton and Tom Epperson, explores the themes of fear, truth, sexuality, and self-discovery. In this moody Southern gothic tale, the main character, Annie, must face great risk in order to find the truth and move forward with her life.

The story revolves around the murder of Jessica, the town debutante, who is killed by her fiancé because she has told him that he is not able to satisfy her, and she has turned to another man for sexual fulfillment. At first, Jessica's killer is wrongly identified, but Annie is not content with surface appearances and feels compelled to look deeper for the truth.

Like many women, Jessica wanted sexual fulfillment but was having trouble finding it. The man who was able to satisfy her was not only socially unacceptable, but psychologically primitive and already married (unavailable). When Jessica called off her affair, Donnie, a troubled and abusive man, hit her and set the stage for his conviction. But it was the clean-cut high school principal who killed Jessica in a fit of rage because she rejected him for his inability to make love to her in a fulfilling way.

The eminent psychiatrist Dr. Carl G. Jung explained that the various characters in a story can be viewed as representing different aspects of one person. From this perspective, we understand that a youthful, eager part of Annie, represented by Jessica, has been "killed." As a result, Annie is emotionally trapped, and can free herself only by discovering the truth about Jessica's murder. When Annie commits herself to confronting the truth she takes great risks with her life, but it is only by meeting this challenge that she can move forward with joy and wholeness.

In real life, true growth is most often accomplished when we are willing to carefully scrutinize the status quo. This includes examining the assumptions, convictions, thoughts, and feelings that we normally do not question—including the dynamics of a relationship.

Throughout history, men have abandoned, punished, or even killed women they no longer wanted, and *The Gift* presents a modern image of this age-old fear: a woman is murdered because her mate cannot stand to hear the truth.

In some ways, this theme continues as an undercurrent of fear in many women. What will happen if a woman tells her lover or husband the truth: that she is sexually unfulfilled? Will he remedy the problem? How? Will he reject her or leave her or find someone else? For many women, there does not seem to be a good solution at hand. No one wants to discuss something if they risk being abused, ignored, or "killed" for it.

What is the solution? Women need to feel comfortable about bringing up the subject of sexual satisfaction, and men need to make them feel safe in order for this to happen. Honesty and openness from both partners is the key to mutually fulfilling sex, and men in particular should be patient and calm when faced with what may feel like criticism. Ultimately, they will be well rewarded for their willingness to listen and respond to their lover's needs.

"It is liberating when a man feels free enough to try all kinds of positions and caresses, discovers what really works, and fine-tunes it to perfection."

—Kim

"In love, like music, the most exciting is often the most simple, but done really well."

—Mark

Freedom

Sexual technique is like musical technique. You must be proficient enough to create the fullest expression of the living act. However, the musician who never gets past technique never really plays music. Similarly, the lover who thinks primarily about technique never really makes love.

Take some time to try what feels right to you and your partner and then let yourself go. Move your hips back and forth, arch your back, let your body loosen up and express your feelings through freer movement, touch, and communication. Try different scenarios. Tune in. You will find your own rhythms and motions.

Be a musician with your lover. Play his or her favorite music and it will become your favorite music, too.

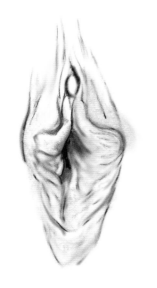

The Clitoris

The clitoris is perhaps the most sensitive point on a woman's body. Most men and many women have no idea how much fulfillment—sexual, emotional, psychological, and physical—can result from stimulating the clitoris fully. When a man learns to fulfill his lover in this way, his own fulfillment is likely to be increased as much as hers.

The key to taking full advantage of her clitoris's sensitivity is controlled use of the tongue, lips, teeth, and fingers. The woman immediately feels the slightest changes in pressure, speed, motion, and direction. Whatever technique one starts with, it is important to sense from the woman's reaction—including the response from her clitoris—what she likes and what she doesn't. For example, during oral sex, if a woman likes what her partner is doing, her pelvis and thighs will relax and she will offer herself to his mouth more. If she experiences discomfort—probably from too much pressure—she will back away or try to push his head away. In this case, the man should lighten his touch. If her clit enlarges, she likes what he is doing. If it shrinks, she doesn't.

Very important: Men should practice on their own fingers to try out the different techniques. He should use his lips and sometimes his teeth (lightly!) to hold his finger so it stays steady while the tongue touches it. Just as increased pressure from his lips and tongue can heighten sensation on his fingertip, it can do so with her clit. If the woman prefers little or no pressure from lips and teeth, the man should practice touching his tongue to his finger without additional pressure from his lips and teeth.

Basic Position

A woman may lie on her back on a bed, her head on or off a pillow, with the man
lying on his stomach, mouth at her genitals. To make it easier, she should bend
her knees and open them as much as is comfortable. Another option is for the man
to kneel on the floor with the woman at the edge of the bed or sofa. This can save trips
to the chiropractor, as extended oral sex can bend the man's neck back excessively.

Some women respond more when their legs are closer together and straight at the knee. If this is the case, it can be helpful for the woman to spread her legs first, with knees bent, and then to straighten and close them later after things are well under way.

Many women like to watch their lover going down on them. This is highly recommended, especially when eye contact can be established frequently.

When a man is going down on a woman, she may prefer to lie still and luxuriate in the experience. Men find it hard to do their best if the woman is bucking hard, but oral sex can be more exciting for both if she moves her hips when she feels the impulse. With subtle movement, she can position her clitoris where she wants it, indicate that she'd like him to lick her vaginal lips for a while, direct him

back to the clit, or focus
on a certain point
(like one side of
the clit or another).
She may also choose
to just move with
the energy she feels
at the moment.
The woman can
always *tell* him
what she wants as well.

Most men like to feel
the woman move.
Her response both
encourages him
and turns him on.

Circles

The clitoris responds quickly when his tongue draws circles on its surface. The smaller the circle, the more his tongue will stimulate the tip of her clit. The wider the circle, the more the tongue will stimulate the base of the clit and the surrounding area. She will likely prefer some of each.

Speed should vary from about one circle per second (one Mississippi, two Mississippi, and so on) to three per second. Circles can be enjoyed for long periods of time, possibly ten or twenty minutes or even hours. If his tongue gets tired, he should pause or try stimulating her with other motions.

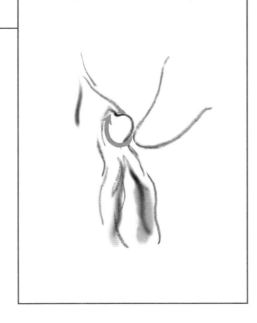

The direction of the circle is very important. Some women respond better to a clockwise motion, while others prefer counterclockwise. Some like both, in which case the man can alternate directions. A combination of three to five clockwise circles, then three to five counter-clockwise circles, continued for several minutes, is usually very effective.

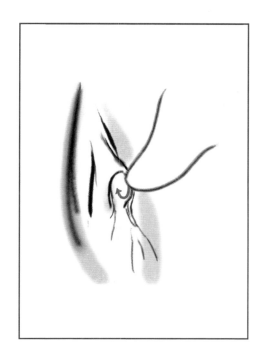 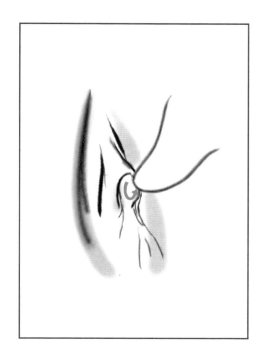

Figure Eights

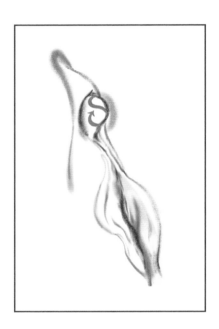

Using his tongue as a paintbrush, the man can draw figure eights on the clit. This requires substantial control, but can be learned quickly. About one figure eight per second

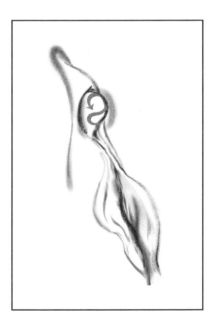

is fine. Alternating clockwise and counterclockwise figure eights will increase her pleasure, and she may discover a preference for one direction or the other. He should keep this up for several minutes if he can.

Up-Down Flicks

The clit can respond dramatically to vertical tongue flicks on its tip. A rhythm of hard flick, pause, hard flick, pause should be tried only after lighter stimulation has been performed. Long, slow flicks, which urge the clit to bend at the tip, can also bring pleasure to the woman. Rapid flicks—light, hard, or alternating light and hard— are especially recommended.

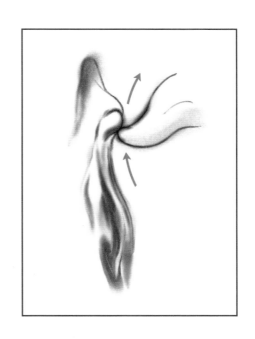

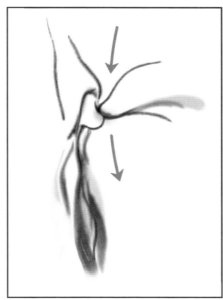

Left-Right Flicks

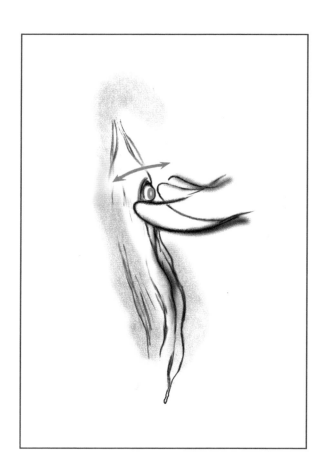

Of all motions, horizontal flicking
produces the most intense results overall.
With practice, the man can develop
great speed (around six left-right flicks
per second). The ultimate motion should
start light and fast, then increase in pressure
slowly until a fair amount of force is applied.
It should then lighten to a feather touch,
and increase again in pressure slowly.
Repeat the sequence in a cycle.

A slow left-right flick is a relaxing motion
for the tongue to make, and so can be used
when other, more demanding motions
have tired the tongue and mouth muscles.

The man can practice as follows:

Look in the mirror. Put the tip of your tongue just
in between your lips, with your teeth parted
and your lips curled slightly inward.
Move your tongue back and forth,
as if licking your lips, and then
slowly restrict the motion to about
one-quarter inch of either side
of center. Feel the motion on your
fingertip. When making love, moving
your tongue from one corner of your mouth
to the other will produce one reaction, while
moving only a small amount will produce a different one.

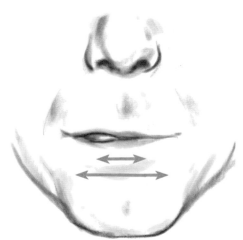

Lips and Teeth

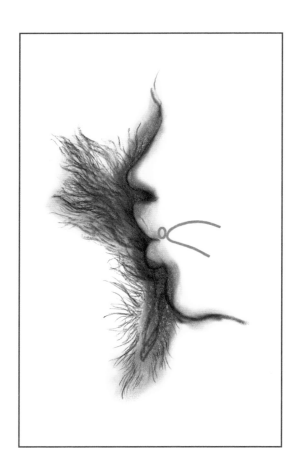

The lips and teeth are useful for creating different sensations in the clitoral area, resulting in maximum arousal, erection of the clit, and ultimately orgasm. Without using the teeth, the lips can be placed around the clitoris to bring the tongue closer. Slowly sucking the clitoris into his mouth, the man should circle his tongue or try left-right flicks. The woman will be more sensitive to figure eights if the man does them while sucking her clit.

In some women, the clit will not be exposed enough to receive the maximum stimulation. If this is the case, the man should place his lips over the clitoral area as described previously. Use the teeth, separated by approximately one-quarter inch (about the diameter of a pencil) to push the folds around the clit away, urging it to come up and out. Doing this while alternating hard-soft with left-right flicking cycles can be incredibly exciting. This requires three simultaneous actions, which may take some practice:

1. pushing folds away with the teeth;

2. sucking on the clitoris lightly; and

3. left-right tongue flicks in hard-soft cycles.

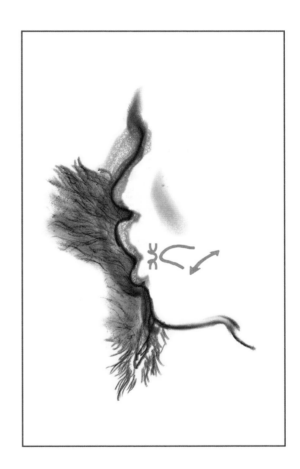

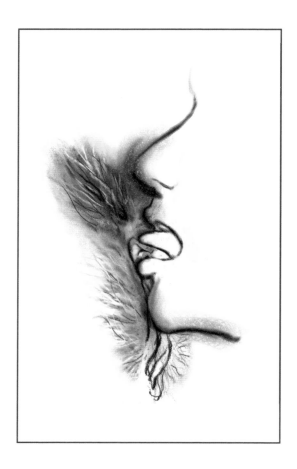

Some women like it when
the man's wet lower lip brushes
against the clit. In this case,
his tongue can make left-right
flicks just above the clitoral area
in between strokes of the lip,
which start at the vagina
and move up and over the clit.

Once the man's tongue and lips
have become well acquainted
with the steps above, he can try
a very light motion with the teeth.

Try this variation: Start by pushing the folds away, then touch the surface of her clit at the base, sliding up until your teeth almost touch. When pushing back down, part your teeth wider as they go toward the base of her clit, just barely touching the surface of the clit. At the base of her clit, try bringing your teeth just a little closer together to urge the clit out, then do circles, figure eights, and flicks.

The important thing is to find out what your partner likes most. Tune in to her and try everything. What she likes most, do more of. If she doesn't respond to a particular motion, abandon it and move on to another.

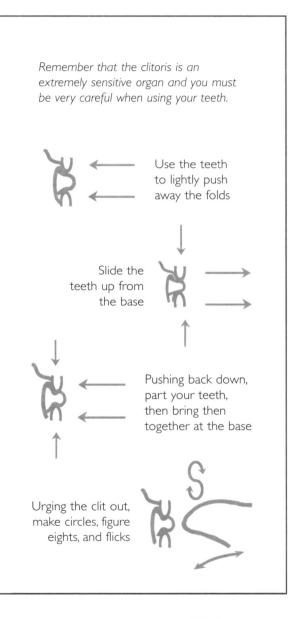

Remember that the clitoris is an extremely sensitive organ and you must be very careful when using your teeth.

Use the teeth to lightly push away the folds

Slide the teeth up from the base

Pushing back down, part your teeth, then bring then together at the base

Urging the clit out, make circles, figure eights, and flicks

Clitoris Twitching

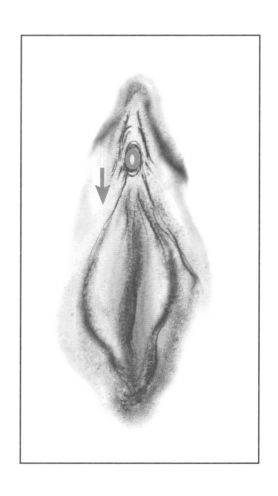

The clitoris can move, sometimes to a surprising degree. Women vary, but a large number do have clits that move when stimulated. The movement is often an up-and-down twitching motion in which the clitoris, starting in the normal position, moves down toward the vaginal lips and then back. When the man has his mouth around her clitoris, this motion is clearly felt by the woman. Likewise, her pleasure and intense feeling is clearly communicated to the man.

Twitching can occur from the slightest stimulation or during climax as a series of strong pulsing movements. If the clit is around one-quarter inch at the base, and a pulse movement is one-sixteenth of an inch, then the clit has moved one quarter of its own size. Think of it this way . . . if a penis moved one-quarter its width,

that would be a pretty phenomenal sensation for a man.

(It would be very erotic for a woman to feel a man pulse

this much in her mouth.)

If a man tunes in, he can feel that same thrill when

he feels his lover's clit pulsing or twitching. How does

he get this response?

Almost any caress by the lips, tongue, or a moist finger

can cause the clit to twitch. Drawing circles on the tip

lightly and steadily will probably result in twitching,

at first in a pleasurable reaction and later as she starts

to climax. If the man's touch is too strong, he may miss

the clit's motion or even blur the sensation for the woman.

When the clit starts to twitch, the man should lighten up

so that they can both experience that motion to the fullest.

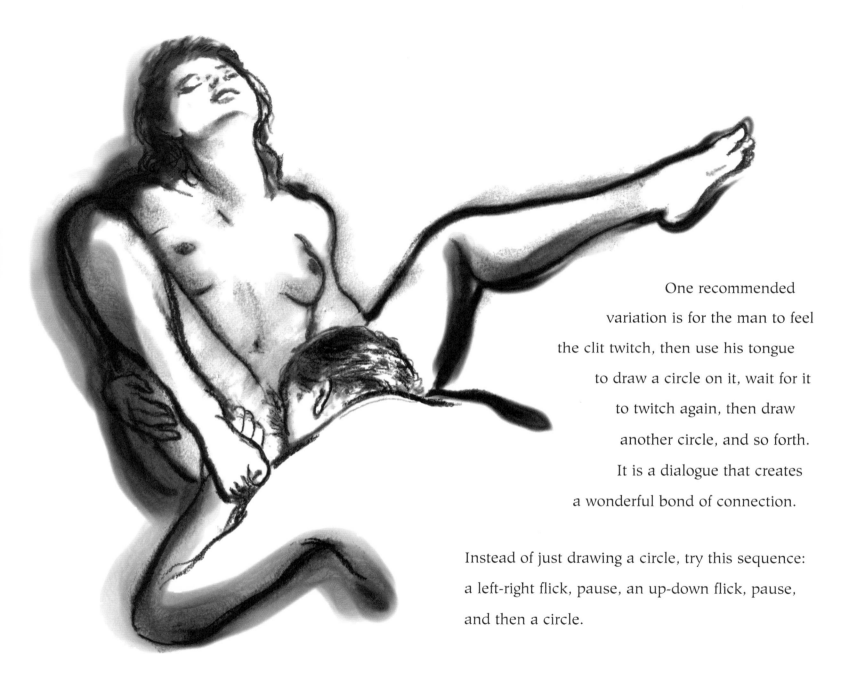

One recommended
variation is for the man to feel
the clit twitch, then use his tongue
to draw a circle on it, wait for it
to twitch again, then draw
another circle, and so forth.
It is a dialogue that creates
a wonderful bond of connection.

Instead of just drawing a circle, try this sequence:
a left-right flick, pause, an up-down flick, pause,
and then a circle.

A sustained light circle on the tip of the clit can be very effective in helping to sustain the orgasm while the clit is twitching.

A man should think of the twitch as being like the contractions of the penis during climax—handle with care but do not ignore.

Some women become increasingly sensitive after one or two orgasms and prefer either a very light touch or no direct stimulation. Others like increased pressure and hard tongue lashing to intensify the feeling. The man must learn what his partner likes, and understand that what she likes may change to a surprising degree over time.

Maintaining some internal finger pressure lifting upward can intensify the twitching in the clit, but too much internal stimulation may obscure the twitching.

Fingers

The man's fingers can be used to assist in oral sex
in a number of ways. One is to spread the lips
of her vagina to gain more complete access
to her clitoris. Massaging the pubic region
by lightly squeezing it in one hand
with a pulsing motion can be stimulating.
The man can try lightly squeezing,
then pushing the pubic region up
toward her breasts. This will enable him
to put her clit more fully in his mouth.
The woman may like it when the man brushes
his fingertips lightly over her lower abdomen,
up and down and side to side, particularly just above
the pubic hair line, extending to the pelvic bones and
toward the navel. A very light touch is recommended.

His fingers can be used inside her vagina to stimulate

both the internal area and the clit from behind.

There are many different areas to touch, starting

at the very outside of the vaginal lips themselves.

A very light presence there can give a woman

a sensation similar to that of his penis entering her.

This can be very exciting at the right time without

the distraction of too much penetration. For most women,

the clitoral area responds best, at least at first, when

very little activity is happening on the inside.

This is because internal stimulation often

distracts from clitoral sensation. When a woman

wants internal stimulation, it is best to start slowly

with one finger touching the vaginal lips

in a circular motion, and then slowly penetrate,

with the fingernail (always cut short, no sharp edges,

and clean) down and the fingerprint side up.

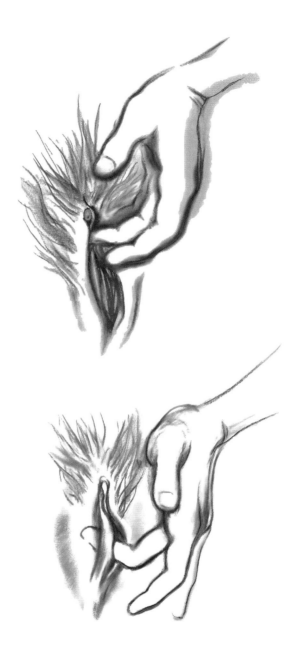

The man should try a slow back-and-forth finger motion just in back of the clitoral area, alternating with tongue motion on the clit. When his tongue is massaging her clit, his finger can be still. Stop the tongue and start with the finger, then repeat for a while.

Keep the finger inside the vagina (not too deep); but don't move the tongue while the finger is in motion. Then, stop the finger motion and begin with the tongue. Simultaneous tongue and finger stimulation can be fantastic for the woman but the man must find the right time for it. He can ask her to touch his shoulder when she wants both together, or she might push down on his finger with her body, asking for more.

When the woman is lubricating and/or enough saliva
is present, two fingers can be inserted, fingerprints up.
Curling the first and second fingers toward you and
alternating their movement can be very stimulating.

A man may practice as follows:

Hold your first and second fingers vertically in front of your face.
Bend them slightly (a "come hither" or curling motion with
two fingers). Like two legs upside down, have them "walk"
toward you one at a time, first the first finger, then the second.

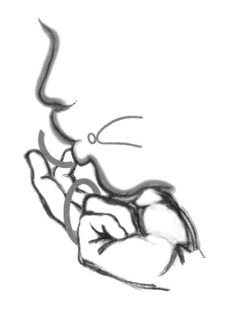

After a few minutes (if not considerably longer) of clitoral stimulation, insert two fingers into her vagina deep enough so that the first finger joints are inside but not the second. Curl the fingers so that your fingertips touch the area in back of the clitoris. Pushing up lightly, move your fingers, one at a time, pushing the clitoris into your mouth. Feel for her most sensitive spot (sometimes called the G-spot), and maintain alternate finger motions. Continue alternating finger and tongue motions (as described previously). Repeat for a while.

Vigorous tongue and two-finger motions done simultaneously can be used to take her from hot to meltdown if she can stand it.

When her feeling intensifies, the man will move both fingers together by bending at the first and second joints, then straightening and bending, straightening and bending, while sucking on her clit and performing left-right tongue flicks and/or circles.

Side-to-side finger motion is also very effective. This, however, requires the fingerprint side of the finger to face either left or right. Turn your right hand so the palm faces left. Insert one or two fingers. Move rapidly left to right, so the spot in back of her clitoris is being touched. You will probably receive plenty of cues from your partner when you get it right. Try different tongue motions on her clitoris while you do this, and abstain for five or ten seconds from clitoral stimulation from time to time to heighten sensitivity.

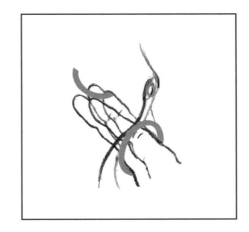

Some women prefer to climax with no vaginal stimulation, while others want it. Most will climax without it, but many have trouble when there is both internal and external activity going on. When in doubt, remove your fingers so she can come, unless she indicates otherwise—such as by moving your hand back toward her vagina.

Anal Stimulation

Some women are driven to new heights of arousal
when anal stimulation is coupled with oral caressing
of the clitoris. There are several things for the man to keep
in mind, including always using a water-soluble lubricant
on the little finger, preferably putting some in the anus
before lovemaking begins.

The man should try the following:

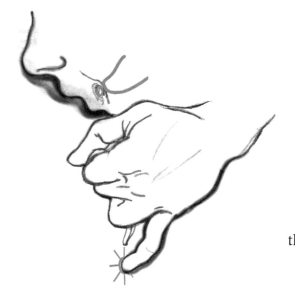

Put some lubricant on your little finger,
then place it against her anus,
but not inside, when you start going
down on her. When the time comes,
later on, slide your finger in without breaking
the flow. Remember, your nails absolutely must

be well trimmed and smooth. Also note that fingers
(or indeed anything) used in the anus must be thoroughly
washed with warm soapy water before entering the vagina,
due to a risk of infection.

The first time you try this, use your mouth on her clitoris
for ten or fifteen minutes, add the use of your fingers
in her vagina for another ten to fifteen
(don't let her come too fast), then take
your fingers out and make her come. Just as
she starts to really come, do the following:
fold your fourth finger down, palm to the side.
Simultaneously insert the first and second fingers
into her vagina and the fifth into her anus in
a slow, steady, determined motion until maximum
penetration is achieved. Just hold your hand there
to fill her while she comes in your mouth.

When in doubt, ask your partner before you try it.
She might want to douche anally first, although
when using lubrication and your little finger,
it generally won't be messy.

For more intense activity, the first, second,
and fourth fingers can be moved in and out
penis-style and/or side to side rapidly
and vigorously while she is coming,
or even before.

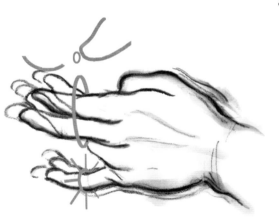

Another approach is to leave
the three fingers inserted
(as described previously)
well before climax is achieved,
using your fingers to fill her and
your tongue to excite her until climax.

Then use either no finger motion, side-to-side

finger motion, or in-out finger motion,

whichever pleases her most.

Take care to find out how much intensity

she wants from the movement of your fingers

and your tongue: just a light presence,

mild motion, or very vigorous action.

Start light and build until you know what

she likes. When in doubt, just ask her

"How's this?" or "Too hard?" or "Softer?"

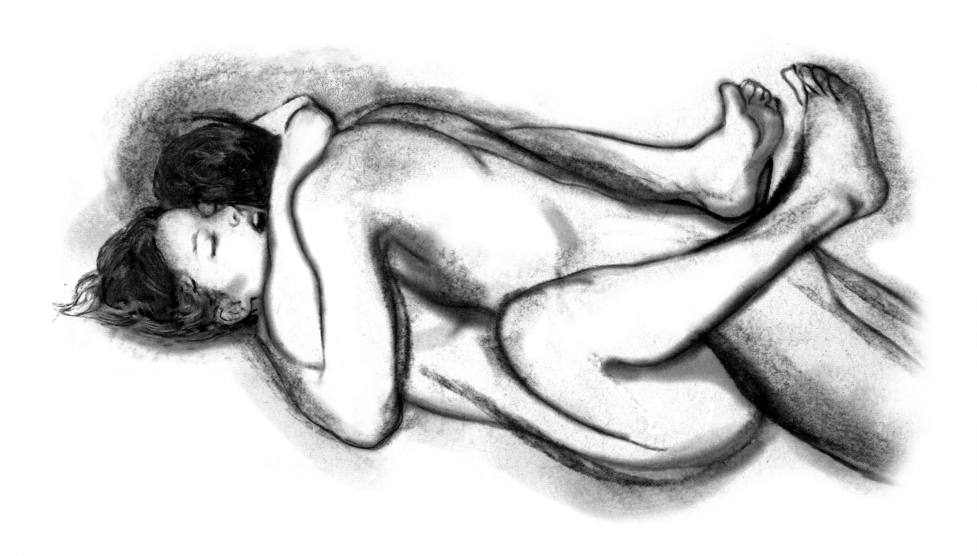

Entering after Oral Sex

Sometimes, a woman will want her partner inside her while or just after she comes. Other times, she may want to rest for a few minutes. Either way, her experience of the man's entry is likely to be far more intense after a long period of great oral sex than without it.

If condoms are used (recommended for all but committed relationships), it is suggested that he put the condom on after going down on her. Many condoms become uncomfortable when they dry out.

The man should read the following carefully:

After coming in your mouth, she may like a combination of being held closely and having vigorous intercourse during which she really feels your penis inside her and the strength of your body on top of her. Now that her G-spot is hot, use your penis to continue stimulating this spot.

Suggested positions include:

1. Missionary position, except the man places his hands under her buttocks to pull them up so the head of his penis can stroke her G-spot.

2. The woman lies on her back and raises her legs in the air while the man holds her legs and strongly penetrates her with his penis, stroking her G-spot as he withdraws and enters.

3. The woman lies on her left side; the man gets on his knees and lifts her right leg while her knee is bent. He enters her sideways so that his right leg touches her pubic area lightly and his penis strokes her deeply— from her vaginal lips, past her G-spot, to full penetration. Then, the man begins what for him are up-and-down movements of the penis, while maintaining full penetration. For the woman, these will be side-to-side movements of a highly exciting nature.

Caressing Her Breasts, Nipples, Etc.

Caressing the woman's breasts and nipples during the previously described activities can be extremely stimulating— and can help bring her to new heights. The man should try rolling her nipples between his first and second fingers. Massaging her breasts upward lightly but with quiet strength can be stimulating, depending on the woman's desires. Lightly touching her nipples while his tongue excites her clitoris can be great for her.

Men: Use your fingers to caress her face and
mouth while you go down on her. She may want
to suck on your fingers, especially when the
fingers of your other hand are inside her.

Pulling her buttocks apart slightly when
you go down on her opens her up more
and helps prepare her for vaginal entry.

The man simply has to see what works
for his partner. Every action should
be accompanied by the thought
"Does this work?" She will answer—
with words or with body language—
"Yes," "No," "Maybe if you do it softer
(or harder)," and so on.

Repeated or Sustained
Oral Orgasms

Many women are so blown away by climaxing in a man's mouth the first time that they can't take any more right away. After some experience with this type of lovemaking, most women find that they can come again and again if the man lightens the pressure of his tongue when she climaxes and then goes very slowly and gently for a while, perhaps avoiding direct clitoral contact.

Men: At this time, try drawing circles with your tongue around the clit but not touching it.
Try sucking on her vaginal lips and licking them.

Look into her eyes if you can,
to show her that you are
really there for her, while
keeping your lips around her clit.
Slowly, gently, with plenty of
lubrication from her own juices,
begin softly to draw slow circles
with your tongue on her clit,
just barely touching it.

You might need to avoid touching her
with your lips and mouth for a bit,
in which case you can stick out
your tongue a little to maintain contact
with her clit until she is ready for more.

Turbo Tongue

This technique is one of the most intense forms
of oral excitement for some women. In order to use
this technique, the man should do the following:

Put the palms of your hands on her inner thighs
just on either side of her vaginal lips and gently
pull them apart. Put your mouth around
her clitoral area and suck it up and out,
away from her body. Your face
will not be touching her body.

Now, draw circles or figure eights, or do left-right flicks, with your tongue on her clit, keeping it sucked out away from her body. The success of this technique depends a lot on your ability to pull the clitoral area away from her body without hurting her as well as on your ability to suck and move your tongue simultaneously while you breathe.

Man Inside

So much has been written about intercourse that most discussion would be redundant, but the following pages reflect some favorite positions.

The most important fact is that each woman has her own preferences, which may change over time or from moment to moment.

A man tends to think in a linear way—that is, in and out. A woman tends to experience in a circular way—around and around. A penis going straight in and out of the vagina may lead to mutual satisfaction, but it tends to be much more effective when coupled with motions that reflect an arc or a circle.

The Favorite Way

This position leads to almost immediate orgasm,
and can be repeated until she either passes out
or can't take it anymore. The caveat is
that the man does very little work
so is likely to have energy left over
(provided he doesn't come),
while she is more than satisfied.

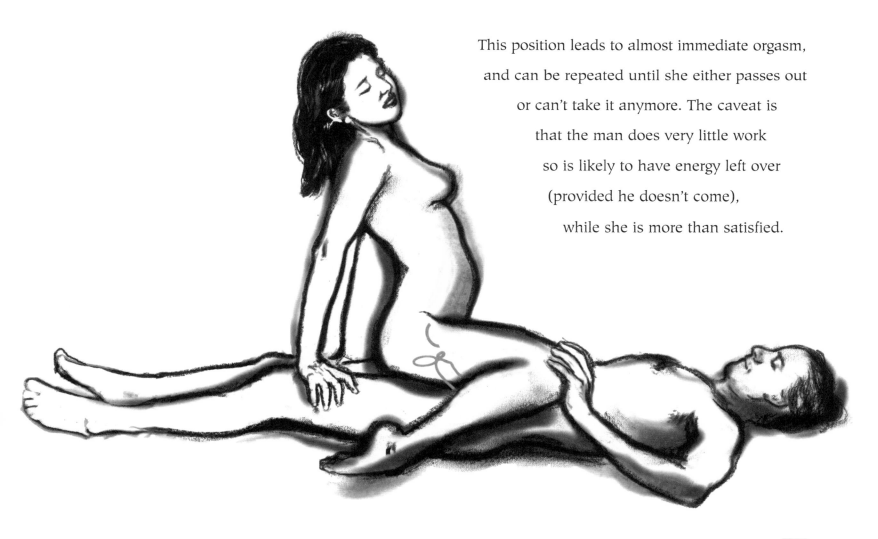

The man lies on his back. The woman straddles him,

with his penis at her vaginal lips but not very far inside.

His penis is pointing away from his face. She supports

herself with her arms, hands on the mattress, body able

to rock back and forth. Her knees will move back and forth

as she rocks. The idea is for his penis to come out of

her vagina, touching her clit as she rocks back; then,

his penis slides back in as she rocks forward.

The man may feel that he is going in and out, but the woman

feels the penis moving in an arc.

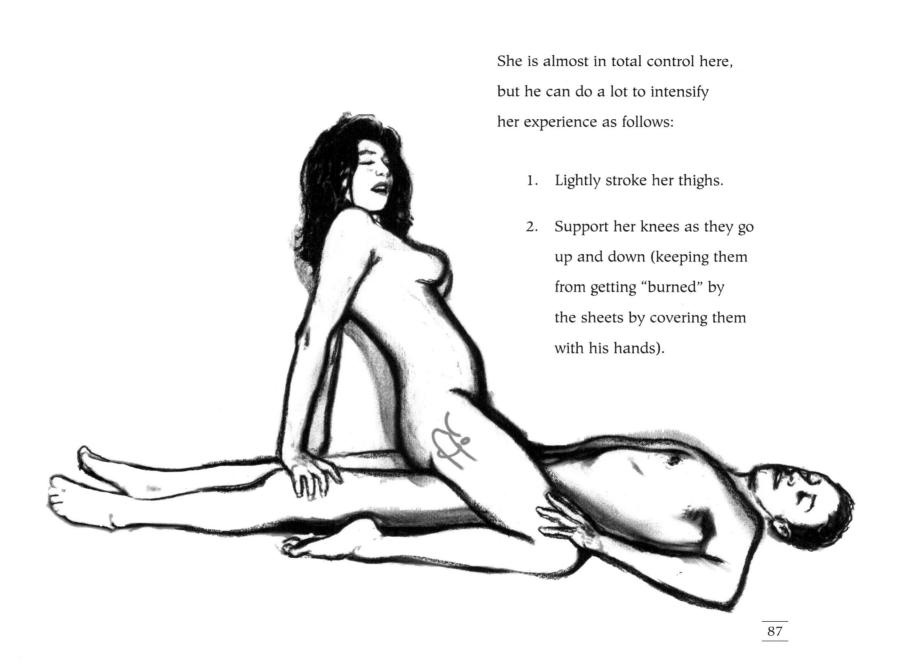

She is almost in total control here, but he can do a lot to intensify her experience as follows:

1. Lightly stroke her thighs.

2. Support her knees as they go up and down (keeping them from getting "burned" by the sheets by covering them with his hands).

3. Touch her clit with his (well-lubricated) thumb, moving it in a side-to-side or circular motion.

4. Touch or squeeze her nipples (ask her how hard) and breasts.

5. Put his hands on her buttocks to support her forward motions (but let her move backward—he might be tempted to keep her forward with his penis in). She may come hardest with his penis only partly in. He will like it best if she pushes her pelvis forward and down so his penis is fully inside.

A nice compromise is for her to do what she wants until she comes, and then please him by moving forward and down so he is fully inside her.

It is key for him not to think about controlling here. He should let the woman move freely and follow her movements. This position is for her to experience and explore; she can find her own rhythm, guiding his motion as she moves. She may find bending back with his penis still inside her most pleasurable.

His penis does not have to go in very far to make her climax this way. It may be best to have only partial penetration most of the time in this scenario.

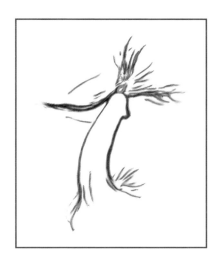

Staying In and Moving

When he is on top and fully inside her, she feels pressure on her clitoral area. He stays fully in and holds her buttocks, one in each hand. He may need to put a pillow on her shoulder to avoid squashing her neck, breasts, or other areas.

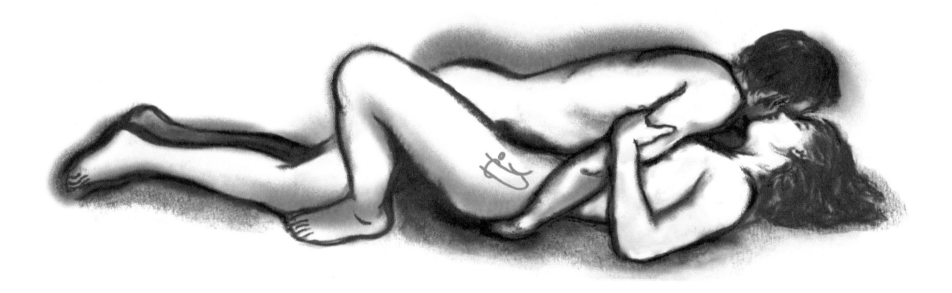

Moving his hips and her buttocks, he makes the tip
of his penis follow an arc that goes either side to side
or up and down. It is best to do some of each.
All the while, he tries to keep
pubic pressure on her
clitoral area, so she feels
filled on the inside
with an arcing motion
while her clit is feeling
an up-and-down or
side-to-side motion.

Lots of variations can be tried, but
the combination of close body-to-body
contact with no in-out motion creates a lot
of heat and lubrication, so when in-out
motion is started later, it's very exciting.

He can also move
his pubic area up
and forward, which
tends to expose
her clit. This makes
the pubic contact
more intense.

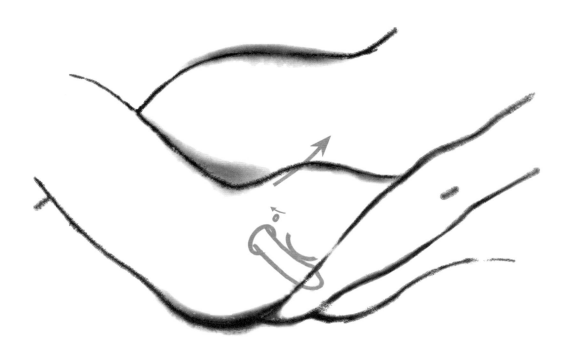

If she likes anal stimulation, he can put a well-lubricated finger (try the little finger, nail well-trimmed) in her anus and leave it there while keeping his penis fully inside her, making no in-out motion. This will make her feel extra "filled" while he moves side to side or up and down (keeping fully inside her). If she starts to come this way, he can wiggle the finger in her anus. Women: Tell him whether you like it—it all depends on your personal preferences.

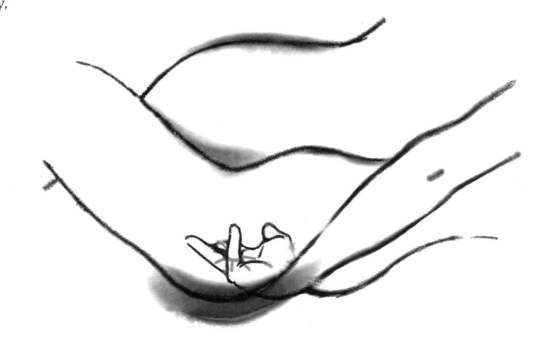

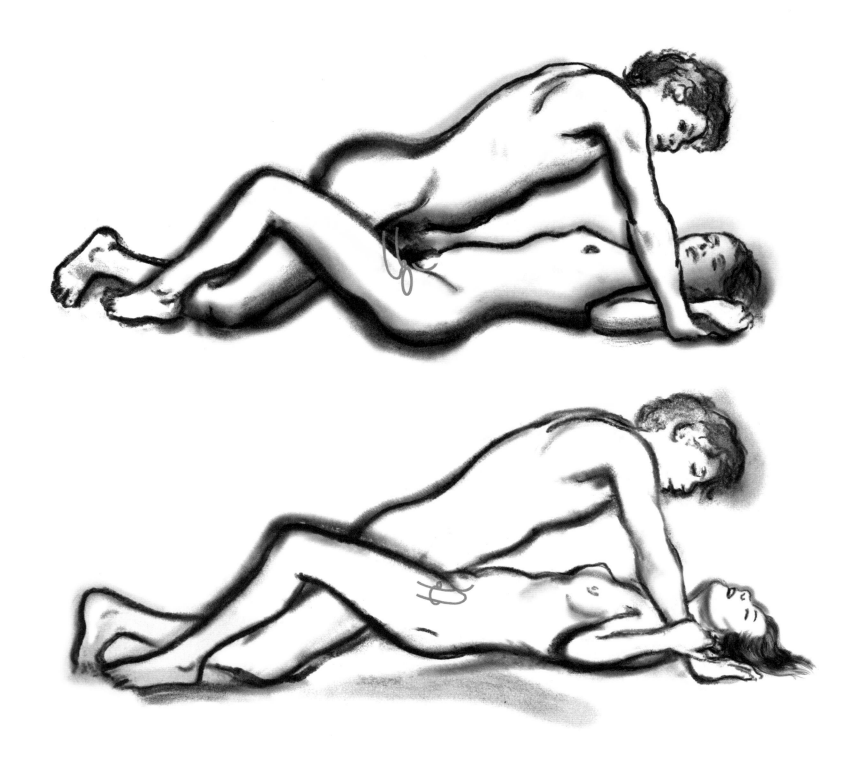

Touching the Clit with the Penis

The man is on top, supporting himself with his arms.
She opens her legs. He takes his penis out of her
and touches its tip to her clit, so his penis is now
pointing straight down toward the mattress. This
requires him to lean forward, raising his hips.
He then strokes her clit, inserting the tip of his penis
in between her vaginal lips and pushing forward,
arcing the tip upward, stroking the G-spot if possible.
He can stay inside and do some up-down and
side-to-side motions, maintaining pubic contact,
then pulling out and stroking the tip of his penis
against her clit again, penis pointing straight down.

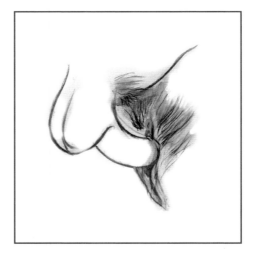

Rear Entry with Him Not Moving

He kneels on the bed; she is on all fours or kneeling
with arms braced on the headboard. The tip of his penis
is inserted in her vagina. He remains still and she moves
the way she wants—side to side, up and down, in and out,
whatever she desires. She can reach around and ask him
to move when (and if) she wants to. This position
is one in which the couple does not have
eye contact, so verbal communication
is important. Listen to her. Some women
are afraid of being hurt by rear entry.
This scenario removes the fear
because she determines the angle,
depth, speed, and force of entry.
He must be careful not to betray her trust
by thrusting too hard, as he might hurt her.

Woman on Top, G-Spot Stroking

The woman is on top, leaning forward so his penis
is touching the upper area of her vagina, around
the G-spot. His penis is pointing toward his chin.
She rotates her pelvis forward and back so that
the tip of his penis massages her G-spot.
This is effective only if the woman's
G-spot is accessible with this geometry.
She will thrust her pelvis forward
and up, causing the tip of his penis
to stroke the desired area.

He can grab her buttocks and assist
her thrusting and moving back.
His touching or squeezing her nipples
while she thrusts is erotic to some women.

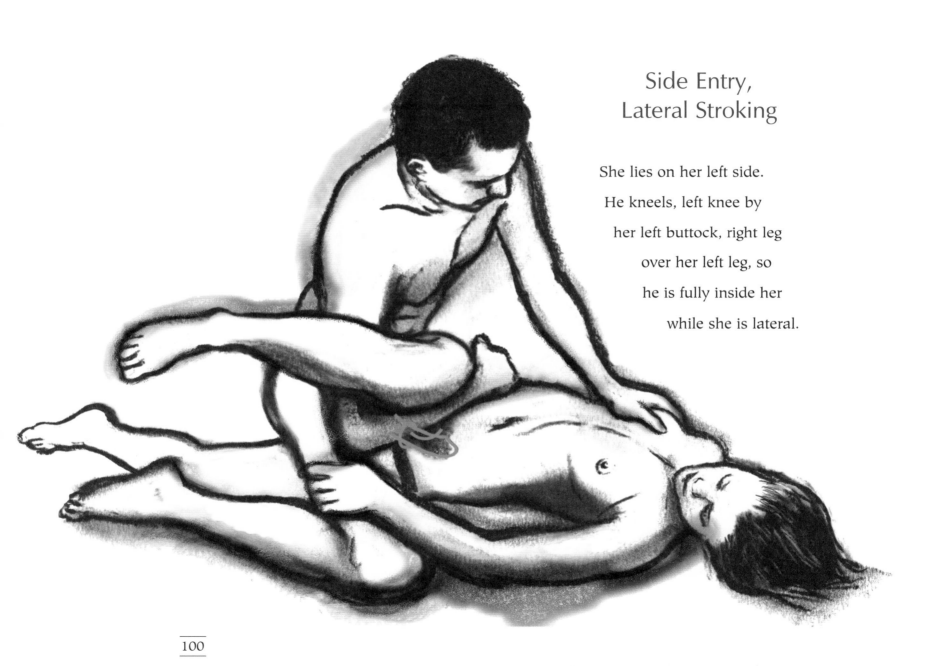

Side Entry, Lateral Stroking

She lies on her left side.
He kneels, left knee by
her left buttock, right leg
over her left leg, so
he is fully inside her
while she is lateral.

He then moves so that the right side of his penis tip strokes the top surface of her vagina, from the G-spot to possibly the opening of the cervix. He should push his pelvis forward to maximize penetration and arcing motion.

He may want to hold her right leg up a little to facilitate deep entry and make arcing movements easier. She may want to touch her clit, as he may not be able to reach it conveniently in this scenario. His left hand may hold her right shoulder; he may touch her nipples; or he might allow her to suck a couple of fingers. The boundaries of imagination are the only limits here.

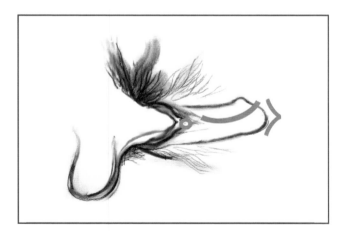

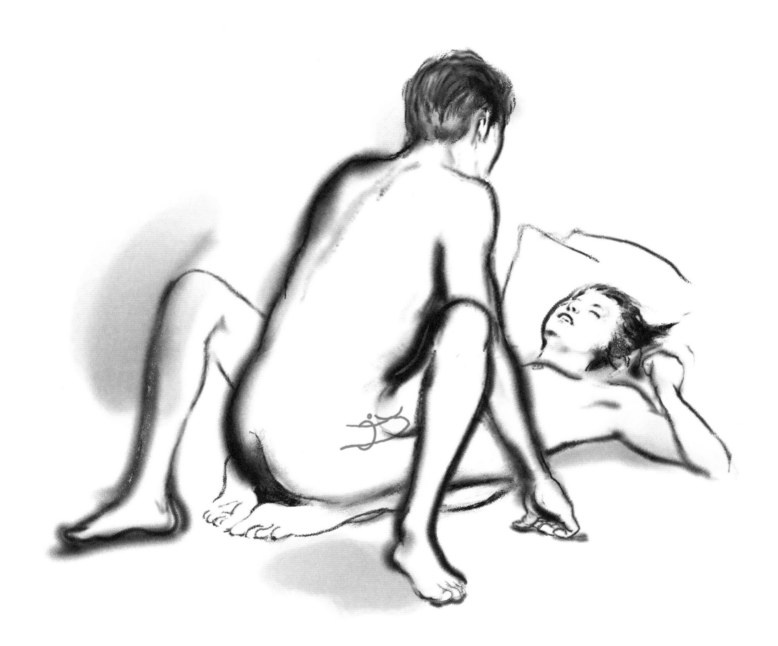

Ultra-Fast G-Spot Massage

He kneels between her legs, with his penis inside her and angled at an upward slant. She lies on her back, knees bent, legs apart, providing him maximum access. He lightly braces himself with his arms, hands resting on the bed or on her breasts. He begins short, fast thrusts that do not enter her fully. The objective is for the head of the penis to rapidly stroke the upper area just inside her vagina's entrance. The man is not so much thrusting as rocking, so that his penis moves only a few inches rapidly back and forth over her G-spot. This move does not require great force, and is fairly easy to do so that it can be maintained for quite some time.

This sustained direct contact on a highly sensitive area creates a lot of heat for her. Normal penetration misses contact in this area, depriving her of critical stimulation. This move also tends to lead to orgasms for the man, as it requires total giving by him, and affords the ultimate view of her, including her face, hair, breasts, waist, genitals, and thighs. Look directly into each other's eyes just before and during climax in this position.

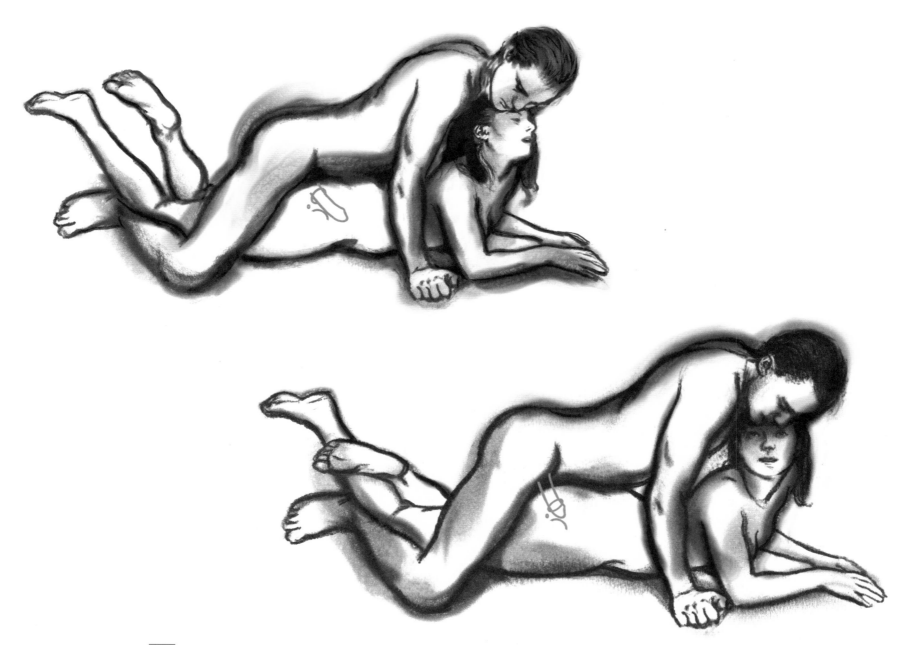

Rear Entry, Riding High

She lies on her stomach; he is on top of her, his legs outside hers
and his arms braced on the bed. He is fully inside her.
As he withdraws, he moves his body forward, so that
the head of his penis strokes her G-spot from above.
He can stroke her G-spot by not fully entering, but
by going back and forth a few inches with his penis
angling down rather than going straight into her vagina.

She can raise her buttocks to facilitate his movement,
rocking to assist in the stroking motion. He can then
achieve full penetration by "riding high" on her back,
so that the tip of his penis touches (or approaches) her cervix.
They can rock back and forth in that position if she likes it.
He must be careful not to hurt her by thrusting too hard or too deeply.
He should start gently and carefully to find out what the limits are.

Head at the Lips

She lies on her back, legs wide apart. He kneels in between
her legs and enters her only enough for the head of his penis
to be partially inside her vaginal lips. He remains still and
lets her control the movement so that the head of his penis
goes from merely touching to being partially inside her.
If she tucks her butt into the bed, his penis will touch her
clit. If she thrusts upward and pulls toward him with her legs,
his penis will enter her further.

In this scenario, the man should be unconcerned
about his penis. Men naturally want to thrust into her
all the way, but that is not what this type of lovemaking
is about. She should be free to do what she wants.
When she is finished, she can let him move freely
as he wishes, so he can reach orgasm.

Her Legs by Her Head

If she is supple enough, she can lie on her back and pull her legs up toward her shoulders. This gives him incredible freedom of motion inside her.

He can move in up-down, side-to-side, and circular motions with ease.
This position can be a real turn-on for him, but should be tried only
if she can accomplish it without discomfort.

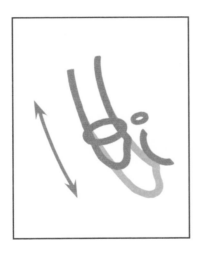 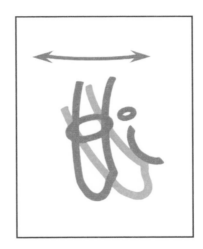 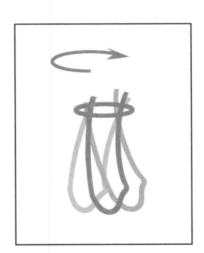

He can hold her ankles (or calves, or thighs) and assist in bracing
her legs in an upright position, or further back if she can manage it.

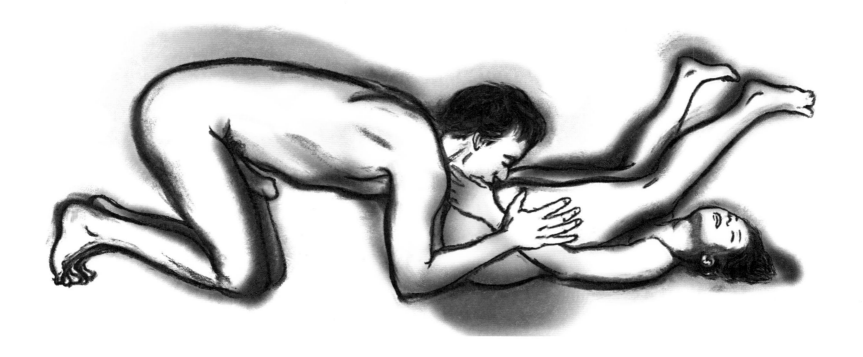

A great variation is for him to move in her freely, then withdraw and quickly start to suck her clit (see previous chapters). He can then enter her again after she is highly excited or comes once or twice. This position requires a quick and smooth movement.

When he is inside her in this position, her clit is not expecting any attention. Taking her by surprise can bring about some amazing results. This position lends itself to an easy transition from him inside her, to her clit in his mouth, and then him inside her again.

She Watches, He Doesn't

She is sitting on a couch or soft chair, watching an erotic movie. He is going down on her softly, so she gets aroused but won't climax too fast. He intensifies by sucking her clit harder when she starts to come (see previous material on oral sex).

This scenario is likely to provide only passing enjoyment, with little long-term attraction. It can be a fun and surprising momentary turn-on, but probably nothing more.

113

She Lies on Top

He lies on his back; she lies flat on top of him, legs extended straight, parted if she wishes. He is inside her, but not too deeply. She lifts her buttocks so that the head of his penis touches her clit, then lowers her buttocks and rotates them forward so his penis enters her. This requires her to use her abdominal and lower back muscles to rotate her pelvis from furthest back (butt up) to furthest forward position (butt down and forward). The illustration shows how this creates a circular motion, a powerfully erotic sensation for her.

This position also allows great body contact and closeness. Being fresh from a bath or shower is a plus, as each will sense the other's hair and body aromas. He can hold her (not impeding her movement, though), stroke her hair, and kiss her face, eyes, and lips.

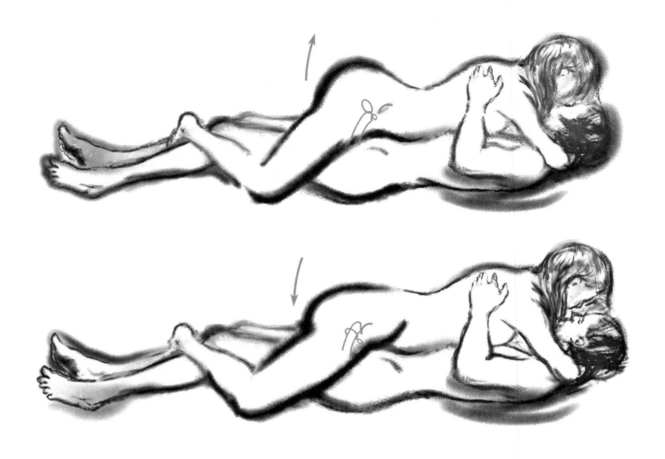

This is a position in which she can achieve orgasm many times. He should be prepared to just lie there while she recovers, if she needs to rest after coming. If he loses his erection, she should help him get hard again and resume.

Viagra

Originally intended to treat sexual dysfunction, Viagra can also make a normally functioning man harder and last longer, which can be very enjoyable for both partners.

Speak with your doctor about getting a prescription—and the proper dosage. Viagra is not appropriate for all men (and in fact can be dangerous for men taking nitrate medications). Be certain to tell your doctor of any health problems you may have and of all medications, prescription and nonprescription, that you are currently taking. While Viagra is generally well-tolerated, sometimes mild side effects do occur, such as headache, upset stomach, and changes in vision. Report any side effects to your physician, who may be able to alter your dosage to eliminate the side effects. If you should experience chest pains, dizziness, or shortness of breath while taking Viagra, discontinue use and see your doctor immediately.

Note that it may not be necessary for the man
to take a whole tablet. A quarter of a tablet
or less may be enough to nicely spark things.

Some women find that Viagra intensifies
their sexual experience. The use of Viagra
is a personal matter to be discussed with
your doctor, and we only wish to say that it
can be wonderful in the right circumstances.

He should not take it unless she is sure
she wants to make love. It is a cruel
and heartless act for her to ask him
to take Viagra and then not want
to make love. Women, be truthful,
appreciate his desire to be the best lover
he can be for you, and give him all you've got in return.

The Preview

He is on top. Just before coming, he withdraws and lets her see the first spurt of his ejaculation, then puts his penis back inside her and finishes coming. This can be a real turn-on for some women. Obviously, this does not work with condoms, and so is generally going to be part of a committed relationship.

He should hold his penis when he takes it out, unless she is fast enough and intuitive enough to reach for him quickly. Simply taking the penis out and having no touch is a big turnoff for him.

She should understand that he probably will not stay hard long after he comes, so she should do her utmost to be there for him when he pulls out and then enters again. He can stay fully inside her and move up against her pubic area to stimulate her clit if

she needs more stimulation to finish.
If she doesn't climax, or wants
to come again, he can go down
on her for as long as she likes it.
Just thinking about seeing his penis
spurt out and then go back
inside her is likely
to make her come
intensely in the
following moments,
if not simultaneously
with him.

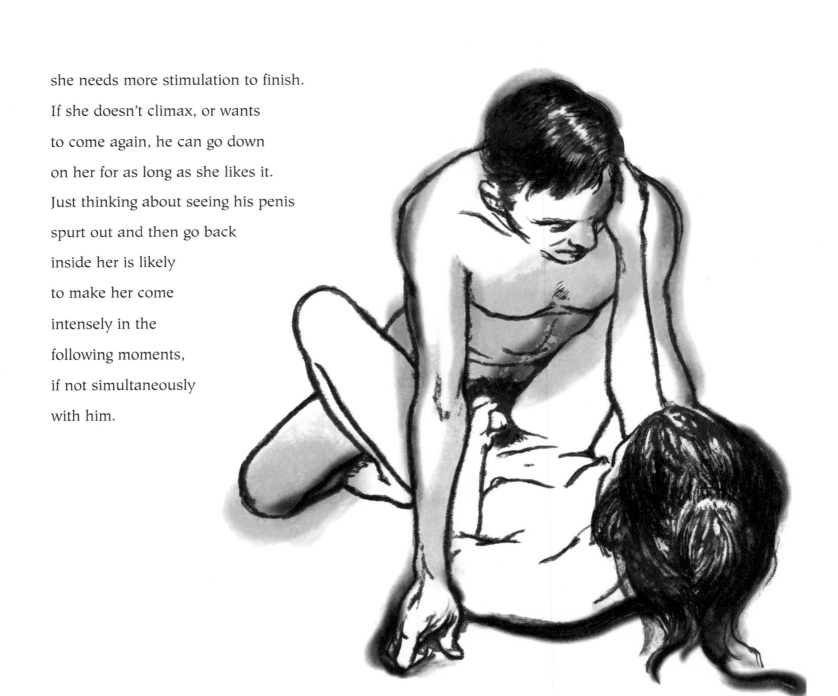

Out of Her Vagina, into Her Mouth

Just before coming, or as he starts to come,

he takes his penis out of her and moves

into position so she can take it in her mouth.

Some women deeply enjoy this. She should be

open and want his juices in her mouth as much

as she wants him to love her juices in his.

This also gives her a chance to taste her own fluids,

which can be especially delicious mixed with his.

This is obviously possible only when the man

isn't wearing a condom, so is best reserved for

a committed relationship or when the good health

of both parties is clearly established.

"Premature ejaculators were the bane of
my existence for most of my adult sexual life.
I felt used, frustrated, and unfulfilled."

—Kim

"Sometimes a woman just makes a man come
quickly, something about her resonates for him
and he can't control his response. It helps
for the man to focus on the woman's pleasure,
even if it temporarily limits his own."

—Mark

Premature Ejaculation

A pattern of premature ejaculation is a concern for many men,
and a fear of ejaculating too soon can lead to a lack of confidence
and avoidance of sex. Women can help their partners
by being sensitive to his anxieties and encouraging him
to relax. One way for him to slow down
is to focus on her first, using his lips,
tongue, and fingers before entering her.

If a man feels he may come too soon,
he can let the woman know and she
can help keep this from happening
by taking his balls in her mouth and
gently pulling down (toward his feet)—
with great care not to bite!

If done well, the result will be to stop him from coming yet keep him hard.
It can be helpful to talk about this before starting to make love.
An agreed-upon phrase or touch from the man can signal her
to take action.

A man should keep in mind how he would feel if, after making love
for a short while, she suddenly stopped. Not good. If a man does climax
too soon, he should remember that she is likely to be strung out and
in need of release. He should forget about his own sexual state of mind
and tune in to hers, and just enjoy making her come until she has
had enough. A real benefit of this approach is the amazing improve-
ment in her moods when sexual frustration is reduced or eliminated.

If premature ejaculation continues to be an issue, men might seek
professional advice, either alone or together with their partners.
A therapist can help a man learn to recognize his approaching "point
of no return" and work toward a slower buildup of erotic sensation.

Communication

For some men and women, it is not easy
to try new ways of making love.
What will my partner think?
Will I do it right? What
will I say if my lover
asks me about it?

Virtually all women
appreciate a man
who wants to be
the best lover
he can be. There are
a number of ways of talking
about doing new things.
The best way is to be honest.

What could be better than saying:
"Honey, I'd like to try some
new things tonight. I hope you
will like them. If there is
something you want me
to change or stop,
just let me know.
You can tap me
on the shoulder
if you want me
to lighten up,
or just tell me
how you
are feeling."

He can say, "I feel that you have a lot more inside you that wants to come out, and I'd like to help bring it out of you."

Putting her first is a good idea. "I'd like to forget about my penis for a little while and concentrate on you. If it's all right with you, could we just take our time and let me feel you more and really get lost in your pleasure?"

If she asks, "What about you?" he might say, "Really getting into your pleasure will turn me on even more, and I think it would be good for me to feel you more."

Humility is a good thing: "I'd like to please you more but I may not be good at it, so I may need your help to find the best ways of giving you more pleasure. Please let me know exactly what you like and don't like. It won't turn me off if you talk to me, I'd really like your help."

Being specific is fine. For example, he may want to try doing circles. He can ask her, "I'm going to try clockwise first. Then I'll try counterclockwise. Tell me which you like better." She will most likely prefer one way better than the other, so why not find out which way?

The woman can help the man by realizing that he is trying to enhance her experience as well as his own. Speaking in a warm way, rather than a critical way, is very important. Encouragement is always going to be more productive than criticism. "No! No! Too hard!" can become "Softer, honey, softer. That's it." Of course, the man has to respond immediately to what she says, just as he would want her to respond if the situation was reversed.

A man should pay close attention to the woman's wetness. It may seem fine to him, but it never hurts to ask, "Would

you like me to use some lubrication?"
A little lubrication can make the difference
between ecstasy and pain. Each woman
has her own individual sensitivity
to being touched in different ways.
A man needs to find out
what works and what doesn't.
When and how much to lubricate
is one of the important questions.
She should—indeed, must—
feel free to speak up and ask for
whatever she wants if the man
has not anticipated her need.
Telling him what you like
and need should be rewarded
by his increased sensitivity to it
the next time around.

"Past abuse—even if it's not directly sexual—
can profoundly affect a relationship,
but can be overcome with love, trust,
understanding, patience, good lovemaking,
and sometimes therapy."

—Kim

"Men are often unconscious about the
deep effects of abuse in women's lives.
This book does not deal with these issues,
but there are fine books and therapists
that can illuminate this vital subject."

—Mark

Abuse

Many women have been abused, either directly
or indirectly, physically or psychologically. In some
instances, a history of abuse may block a woman
physically and emotionally from responding to activities
that would otherwise lead quickly to orgasm. Women with
a history of abuse often benefit from professional help.
However, from personal experience, we can say that
loving patience and caring often allow the woman
to overcome her resistance to feeling pleasure.

Some of the things women find most pleasurable
produce little response the first time they are tried.
Women often need time to trust, to feel secure,
comfortable, and open. Find out what works best now,
but always keep an open mind for the future.

"A satisfying sexual connection
is an essential element
of our physical and
psychological health."

—Kim and Mark

Encouragement

Everyone needs and likes encouragement.
Especially when making love, it is important
to be encouraging, although not at the expense
of the truth. Lying to make someone feel good
ultimately sabotages the relationship.
A woman can say how much she appreciates
his trying to make her feel good. A man
can say how much he likes being close
to her and finding out what she likes most.

Encouragement furthers, whereas criticism
cuts short. A few words of encouragement
each time you make love are a good thing.

"Scratchy doesn't work for me.
I need my man clean, smooth,
and fresh."

—Kim

"If you want to turn her on, do it
on all levels. On is better than off."

—Mark

Clean and Smooth

Most women prefer a man who is clean and freshly shaven.

Some men, especially those with strong body odor, should bathe

just before making love. Many women are far more sensitive to odor

than they will admit, and may turn off to the way a man smells.

Diet can affect body odor, and if you want to know more about this

there is a fair amount in print. Taking certain pharmaceuticals

can also cause unpleasant body odor.

Shaving is much more important than men usually think. Men,

imagine stroking your face and penis with sandpaper. This is what it

can be like for women to make love with you when you need a shave.

Breath is also very important. Bad breath can be caused by many

things, including teeth that need cleaning, diet, not eating or drinking

enough water, and other factors.

Men should ask women to speak up if there is any unpleasant body odor, bad breath, or whiskers affecting her. A woman can hand her partner the items she thinks he needs, like soap, a toothbrush, or shaving cream. He should just take it, clean himself up, and enjoy the benefits. Have a sense of humor about it and don't let ego get in the way.

Final Thoughts

Making love is an endless mystery and can never be fully explained by illustrations and text. For a man, truly making love to a woman means sensing every vibration in her, so that he can actually feel what she feels. When a man totally fulfills a woman, she can, in turn, totally fulfill him.In this way, sex reflects the emotional relationship.

Sex is best when people are in touch with each other on as many levels as possible. One can be a technically good lover, that is, one can know how to make another person climax, but the best sex happens when a person lets himself or herself go, and it is impossible to say what allows this to occur. We can have great sex with someone we don't even know, or terrible sex with someone we love. The real question is how to combine all the influential elements to give and receive sexual satisfaction.

The answer starts with the desire to find that satisfaction. Regardless of who you are or the state of your relationship, it is a tremendous help to know what to do—how to touch and move with your lover—to maximize pleasure and make the juices flow. Tapping into the realm of animal sexual intensity is a great part of life. Sex is a reflection of the energy of the moment.

This energy changes with the partner and with the moment, and is never the same twice. When a man understands how to make love to a woman, he provides a foundation, ensuring that whatever happens, the sex will almost always be good. And if for some reason it isn't, he will allow it to stop gracefully until the next opportunity presents itself.

Sexual satisfaction cannot be captured in the pages of a book. The suggestions here are meant to begin a dialogue between lovers and help them reach out to each other in their quest for an ever more fulfilling sex life.

This book is ultimately about a commitment to care for our partner, to be sensitive to his or her needs and desires, and to strive to bring out the best in each other. When this promise is lovingly made and honored, we each write our own book on satisfaction.

About the Authors

Kim Cattrall is a two-time Golden Globe and Emmy-nominated actress who has received worldwide acclaim for her portrayal of Samantha Jones in the HBO hit series *Sex and the City*.

Born in Liverpool, England, Kim was raised on Vancouver Island, British Columbia, Canada. When she was sixteen, Kim moved to New York City to attend the American Academy of Dramatic Arts. Upon graduation, Kim contracted with Universal and played opposite Jack Lemmon in *Tribute*. Some of her subsequent film credits include *Mannequin, Masquerade, Star Trek 6: The Undiscovered Country, Big Trouble in Little China, Bonfire of the Vanities, The Heidi Chronicles*, and *Live Nude Girls*. Her stage credits include *A View from the Bridge, Three Sisters, Miss Julie, The Misanthrope*, and *Wild Honey*.

Kim is a founding supporter of the Music Maker Relief Foundation.

Mark Levinson was born in Oakland, California. As a child, he played constantly with the family record player, and went on to become a professional jazz musician on flugelhorn and double bass. He played with many jazz greats, including Paul Bley, Sonny Rollins, Keith Jarrett, and Bill Elgart, and studied North Indian Classical Music with Ali Akbar Khan for many years.

Mark is the founder and CEO of Red Rose Music. An audio icon, he has set standards of excellence in the field since 1971. He assisted Tim and Denise Duffy in founding the Music Maker Relief Foundation, which helps forgotten elderly country blues and folk musicians by offering funding, medical help, musical instruments, and care. Mark provides recording and mastering services to the Foundation when needed.

Index